WITHDRAWN
AND
DONATED
FOR SALE

Learning About Towers and Dungeons

by Leone Castell Anderson
illustrated by Joe Van Severen

 CHILDRENS PRESS, CHICAGO

To my men: Eric, Scott, Jim and Paul

— with love.

Library of Congress Cataloging in Publication Data

Anderson, Leone Castell, 1923-
   Learning about towers and dungeons.

  (Learning about series)
  Summary: Describes some of the world's most famous towers as well as a few dungeons and prisons, and relates historical tales associated with several of the structures.
    1. Towers—Europe—Juvenile literature.
2. Towers—Juvenile literature.   3. Prisons—Europe—Juvenile literature.   [1. Towers.
2. Prisons]   I. Van Severen, Joe, ill.
II. Child's World (Firm)   III. Title.
IV. Series.
D910.5.A5   1982   940   82-9639
ISBN 0-516-06538-6

Copyright© 1982 by Regensteiner Publishing Enterprises, Inc.
All rights reserved. Published simultaneously in Canada.
Printed in the United States of America.
1 2 3 4 5 6 7 8 9 10 R 91 90 89 88 87 86 85 84 83 82

Learning About
Towers and Dungeons

Created by

Have you ever built a castle on the beach? or a tower in your bedroom? Maybe you've climbed a tree and made believe it was a look-out tower. Or you've pretended you were being held captive in a high tower with only one window.

Or, perhaps you prefer dungeons? Deep down below the earth. Down where it's dark and damp . . . and spooky. Who knows what you might find there—maybe even a ghost!

A dungeon was often part of a tower. Some dungeons became famous as torture chambers. Of course, there are not many dungeons left and they're no longer used as they once were used.

But towers abound. Castles have towers. Cathedrals have towers. Many of these towers are in European countries.

There are, however, such towers in other countries. And there are other kinds of towers. Church and clock and bell towers. Skyscrapers. Traffic-control towers. Fire, water, and lighthouse towers.

What makes a tower? A tower is a structure higher than it is around. Sometimes it is square or rectangular. Sometimes it is round. It can be part of a building. It can stand alone.

Long ago, people built towers for defense. From the towers they could drop stones, shoot arrows, and throw spears at their enemies!

These towers, called keeps, were built inside great walls of stone or brick. The keep was used as a look-out. It was also where a nobleman or knight and his family lived within a castle.

If enemies broke down the castle gates, people ran to the keep. There they would be safe. Or there they would make a "last stand."

But the towers were built for reasons other than defense. They were symbols.

The towers on churches and cathedrals said, "We point up to heaven and God."

Other towers said of their builders, "We're rich. We're important. We're powerful."

Dungeons were also symbols of power. And of vengeance.

Some rulers had dungeons beneath every tower of their castles. (Maybe they had lots of enemies!)

Some had secret dungeons. These were cut into the rock below the floor of a tower. They were known as oubliettes (oo-ble-ets'). They could be reached through a trap door in the floor.

Just the thought of being sent to a dungeon made people shiver. They tried to do what was expected. They'd do anything rather than hear, "Off to the dungeon!"

TOWERS OF POWER

Dungeons have existed for hundreds of years but towers have been around even longer. Some towers built 5000 years ago were known as ziggurats (zig'-oo-rats).

A ziggurat was a sequence of levels. Each level was built—one on top of the other. And each level was smaller than the one below it. Some researchers believe the

Tower of Babel

in Babylon was a ziggurat. The Bible tells of this tower.

King Nimrod thought a tower could show his power. His people began to build the Tower of Babel. No matter how high they built, Nimrod wanted it higher. "I will be mightier than God," Nimrod said.

The tower rose into the clouds. Then one day, the people began to speak different languages. They couldn't understand each other. They were scared. They recognized this as punishment from God. Work on the tower stopped. People fled the city. The Tower of Babel fell to pieces.

This tower in Babylon was destroyed and rebuilt a number of times. It was rebuilt for the last time about 600 B.C. Today we can only imagine how it looked. Nothing remains.

Would you believe some towers could be moved around? The

"Belfry,"

used in the Middle Ages, was another name for a siege tower.

It was a two- or three-story tower on rollers. To attack a castle, the tower would be rolled right up to the castle walls. Attackers would climb out of the tower and over the walls. Once inside the castle walls, they would let the drawbridge down so the rest of the army could get in.

A siege tower was built on a wooden framework. Inside was a wooden ladder. The outside was covered with wet animal hides. The wet hides kept the people in the castle from setting fire to the wooden siege tower.

TOWERS OF FAITH

But towers have more often been built to call the faithful to worship. In Islamic countries, a man called a muezzin (mu-ez'-in) climbs a

Minaret

five times a day.

From the balcony on top he calls the followers of Mohammed to prayer.

One famous minaret is the Qutub Minar. It stands in the Red Fort of Old Delhi, India. A Muslim king began the minaret in 1200 A.D.

Qutub Minar is built of red stone. It has inlays of white marble. Verses from the Koran (Islamic holy book) are carved into it.

A climb up the 378 steps of Qutub Minar gives a great view of Delhi, Old and New. You can look out—and catch your breath—at balconies on every level.

The Christian faith inspired many cathedral towers. These towers were supposed to point the way to God. Some people in Ulm, Germany, wanted to build the biggest and most beautiful church ever seen. So they began the

Ulm Cathedral

But problems arose. The foundations weren't deep enough. The tower was only halfway up when it developed cracks.

After 152 years, work stopped. Interest and money had dwindled. So there the cathedral sat for 361 years—its spire a squared-off tower.

Then, in 1892, the tower was finally completed and Ulm's dream came true. Its cathedral has the highest church tower in the world. It rises 528 feet.

Canterbury Cathedral

has been called the "Mother Church" of England. That's because it was first built in 597 A.D. But that first building was destroyed by fire in 1174.

Then a master builder (architect) from France was hired to rebuild it. One day he fell from a scaffold and had to return to France. But his plans for the church were used.

The building went on for 300 years. Canterbury Cathedral, with its three soaring towers, was the first example of Gothic style in Britain.

In the 1300s, Geoffrey Chaucer wrote *The Canterbury Tales*. These were stories about people on a pilgrimage to Canterbury. They were going to the tomb of Thomas Becket.

Becket was a bishop who died rather than give up his beliefs. He did not agree with King Henry II, who wanted to be head of the church. The King ordered Becket killed. King Henry's men murdered Becket in the Cathedral.

Becket is buried beneath the floor of Canterbury Cathedral. Today a plaque marks the spot.

Notre Dame means "our lady" in French. ("Lady" refers to Mary, the mother of Christ.) That's why many great cathedrals in France are called Notre Dame. In Paris,

Notre Dame Cathedral

was built on an island, Ile de Cite, in the Seine River. It was begun in 1163. Work went on for hundreds of years. Two

large square towers were built on the west end. Spires were to be added to these towers. But it took so long to finish the cathedral that the spires were never added.

A famous and beautiful "rose window" is located between the square towers. It is made of stained glass.

Victor Hugo's story, *The Hunchback of Notre Dame,* takes place in this cathedral. The story is set in the 15th century (1400s).

Quasimodo (kwas-ee-mo-do'), the hunchback, was not only misshapen. He was deaf, too. His job was to ring the bells in the cathedral's bell tower.

In those days people were often punished for little reason. This happened to Quasimodo. He was publicly whipped. A gypsy girl, Esmerelda, took pity on him. She brought him water.

Quasimodo remembered that. And when Esmerelda was accused of being a witch and was to be punished, Quasimodo rescued her. He brought her to the bell tower of the cathedral. He thought she'd be safe. (A church was supposed to be a refuge for those who needed it.)

However, Quasimodo's evil boss, Frollo, stirred up the

crowd against the two fugitives. Quasimodo threw down huge stones from the tower. He tried to scare the crowd away. But the crowd set up ladders. The hunchback pushed the ladders from the wall.

Finally Frollo tricked Quasimodo and released Esmerelda to the angry mob. Enraged, the hunchback threw Frollo from the bell tower. Tears rolled down Quasimodo's cheeks. He realized it was too late to save Esmerelda.

Another church tower that has gone down in history is the

Old North Church Tower

From this Boston church tower in 1775, lanterns were hung to signal Paul Revere. Revere alerted the colonists that the British were coming!

The Old North Church and its tower still can be seen today. It was built in 1723. It is Boston's oldest church.

TOWERS THAT WORK

Bell towers are sometimes known as "singing" towers. Bells call people to worship or pray. They ring to warn of danger. And they ring to celebrate good news! The

Leaning Tower of Pisa

is a famous bell tower.

The people in Pisa, Italy, had a lovely cathedral. Next to it they wanted a matching bell tower. Work began on the tower in 1183. Before long, though, it was apparent that the tower leaned. No one knew what to do. The tower sat for several years.

Then three more stories were added. The tower leaned even more. The people of Pisa began to like the lean. They thought the tower was special. It was different. Four more stories were added. The tower was completed in 1350.

Seven bells were hung in the tower. The heaviest ones hung on the side away from the lean.

The top of the tower leans 14- to 16-feet out over the bottom. As years pass, the tower seems to lean more and more. Experts are called in from time to time. They add special supports. The people of Pisa want to preserve their leaning tower.

In early days, many towns put up clock towers. Very few people had clocks at home. The town clock and its bells told them when to rise, when to eat, and when to go to work. It also seemed to say, "Our town is important." There's a clock tower in England that has won fame for its town. It is called

Big Ben

Can you imagine a clock that weighs about five tons? No wonder it is called Big Ben! Big Ben is the clock in the tower of the Houses of Parliament in London, England.

The name Big Ben was first given in 1858 to the great bell that hung in the tower. The bell was named after the Commissioner of Works. Sir Benjamin Hall was his name. And he was a large man.

The next year the clock was put into service. People started calling it Big Ben, too. It was first wound by hand. Can you imagine what a big job that was? Now the clock runs by electricity.

The sound of Big Ben's chimes is known all over the world! And the clock can be seen for miles. There are four clock faces—one on each side of the tower.

Sometimes towers are designed to be monuments or memorials. The

Eiffel Tower

is one of these.

A French engineer, Alexandre Eiffel, created the Eiffel Tower. He built his tower for the Paris International Exposition of 1889. It was to celebrate the centenary of the French Revolution.

Eiffel used new methods to build the tower. He used the then-new material, steel. The workers put together 12,000 different parts. They used 2½ million rivets. It took them 17 months. They worked at dizzy heights.

The tower was not an immediate hit. At first the people thought the 984-foot steel skeleton was ugly.

Slowly, though, the "monstrous" tower became a favorite. Sightseers flocked to it. Within a year they'd paid for the million-dollar monument.

Today people like to view the countryside from the tower's platforms. People can have a meal there. They can even go to the theater there! People read the time and temperature from the tower's clock and thermometer. At night they watch its beacon light the sky.

A television tower now adds 59 feet to the Eiffel Tower's height. (And it adds a 20th-century touch.)

Towers aren't built for defense or protection anymore. People are not trying to reach heaven by building towers. But towers still say, "We're important." And they still rise high in the sky to get attention. One modern tower built in the 1940s was the

Johnson Wax Research Tower

Think of it next time you help wax the floor or furniture. Many ideas about new ways to clean come from the tower.

The Johnson Wax Tower was designed by the American architect, Frank Lloyd Wright. He saw the building as a tree. The trunk was the central core of the tower. Its roots (foundation) went deep into the ground. Its branches (floors) spread out from this trunk (core), without other support.

And that's the way the tower was built. This new way of building came to be known as "core and cantilever."

The tower's outer walls let in lots of light. They have bands of brick and glass tubes. A winding inner stairway takes you to the laboratories and offices on each floor.

Castle and cathedral towers were built high and mighty. The builders wanted people to notice their towers. Two modern apartment towers on the Chicago River in Illinois were designed to catch your eye, too. They're different. They look like tall ears of corn. The

Marina Towers

are 60 stories high. They, too, are of "core and cantilever" design.

Both the towers are round. The apartments inside are like slices of pie. The widest end of each slice has window walls overlooking the city. The rooms become narrower toward the middle of the building. The center core has elevators to reach the apartments.

There are rounded balconies outside every apartment. These balconies make the towers look like corn cobs.

Communication is another purpose for modern towers. Some towers have antennas that pick up high frequency waves. The waves are used by our radio and television stations. One such tower is the 620-foot

GPO Tower

in London.

It was built in 1965. This communication tower is on top of London's General Post Office. Most of the floors in the tower have equipment in them. But there are galleries where visitors can get a great view of London.

Television and radio stations also transmit from on top of the

Sears Tower

in Chicago, Illinois.

At 110-stories high, Sears Tower is the tallest tower in the world. It rises 1,454 feet (443 meters) high.

Construction of Sears Tower began in 1970. It took four years to complete. Over 1,500 people worked on the tower.

An enclosed skydeck on the 103rd floor gives visitors an expansive view of Chicago. The skydeck can be reached by express elevators in 55 seconds!

Besides the skydeck, the tower includes office space, stores and restaurants.

Sears Tower is built of 76,000 tons of steel. It contains over 16,000 bronze-tinted windows. And the building has more than 144,000 light fixtures!

A tower with a revolving restaurant is the

Berlin TV Tower

This tower reaches up 1200 feet. You can see all sides of Berlin while you munch bratwurst!

DUNGEONS OF LONG AGO

Towers reach high into the sky. Some also go down below the ground. One famous tower with dungeons deep down is the

Tower of London

The history of this famous tower goes back to 1066. That's when William the Conqueror fought the English and won. He built the Tower of London to protect his new kingdom.

Many kings followed William. They all added to the Tower. They built walls, moats, and other buildings. And they built dungeons.

Many stories have been handed down about famous people held captive in the dungeons of the Tower of London.

There's the story of Edward V. At age 12, Edward was to be crowned king. But his uncle wanted to be king. It is said that the uncle had both Edward and his younger brother put to death in the tower apartments. No one really knows whether the story is true. But the uncle did become King Richard III.

Henry VIII came along in the 1500s. He gave the Tower of London a really bad name. He sent his enemies to the dungeons. (And he had a lot of enemies!) Most of them never came out alive.

Even Queen Elizabeth I stayed in the Tower for a time. She was sent there by her sister, Queen Mary.

The last prisoner to be kept in the Tower was locked up in 1941. Rudolph Hess, a Nazi leader, was held there for four days. Then he was transferred to the prison at Mytchett Place in Aldershot, England.

More than prisoners were kept in the Tower of London. Leopards, bears, and even an elephant once lived there! Henry III started the Royal Zoo. However, when a lion took a nip out of a soldier in 1835, the then-king said, "Enough!" And that was the end of the Royal Zoo.

Part of the Tower of London was and still is a museum. You can go there to see old suits of armor and old guns. Some were used by kings in the past. And the crown jewels are kept in the Tower of London.

A notorious castle dungeon was the

Dungeon at Chillon

which also stands as a museum today. It contains reminders of a violent past.

Chillon's past began in the 13th century. That was during the time of Duke Peter II of Savoy. Duke Peter's men threw people into the dungeon on the slightest excuse. They tortured their prisoners until they confessed to things they'd never done.

Father Francis Bonivard was held prisoner in Chillon during the 16th century. He disagreed with the Duke about religion. Bonivard was chained to a pillar in the dungeon. During his six years there, he was tortured. When patriots took the castle, Bonivard was freed.

Lord Byron, a poet, learned of this story. He wrote a poem about it nearly 300 years later. It's called "The Prisoner of Chillon."

The Castle of Chillon still stands today. It's on a rock island about 10 yards off the shore of Lake Geneva, Switzerland. It's open to tourists, so you can visit it—if you dare.

The most feared and hated dungeon in France was the

Bastille

In the 14th century the Bastille was a gate to Paris. It was a fortress built on the Seine River. The strong walls were built to protect Paris from the English and from pirates.

A stout castle was added—a castle with dungeons. Soon the Bastille was all dungeon. The people of Paris felt they needed to be protected *from* the Bastille.

All it took to be thrown into the Bastille was a letter with the king's seal. Members of the ruling class managed to get some of these letters. They used them to put their enemies into the Bastille. Once people were put into this dungeon, they very seldom came out.

The Bastille was dark and dirty. The floors were covered with moldy straw. There were bugs and spiders and lice and mice. A ledge in the stone wall was a bed.

There were iron rings in the wall. One end of a chain was attached to these rings. The other end was attached to iron bands on the prisoner's waist or neck or legs.

And then there were the secret dungeons. In these pits there was no light and very little air. They were cold. Sometimes water seeped in from the river.

You can see why the people of France destroyed the Bastille. On July 14, 1789, mobs of people marched on the hated prison. "Liberty!" they shouted. "Equality! Fraternity!" And they tore down the Bastille. It was the beginning of the French Revolution.

The people of France still celebrate Bastille Day on July 14. It's like the Fourth of July in the U.S. Stones in the pavement now mark the spot where the Bastille once stood.

Dungeons are no longer places of execution and torture. Some are museums, open to sightseeing. Many are gone and forgotten.

But towers still exist. Towers light and airy. Towers strong and sturdy. Towers still reaching upward to the skies. There are towers all around you. You just have to look up to see them!

INDEX

Babel, Tower of, 13
Bastille, 44-45
Bastille Day, 45
Becket, Thomas, 19
Belfry, 14
Berlin TV Tower, 38
Big Ben, 27
Byron, Lord, 43
Canterbury Cathedral, 19
Canterbury Tales, The, 19
Cathedral towers, 6, 17
Chaucer, Geoffrey, 19
Chillon Dungeon, 43
Core and Cantilever, 30, 33
Edward V, 40
Eiffel, Alexandre, 28
Eiffel Tower, 28
Elizabeth I, Queen, 40
Esmerelda, 20-22
French Revolution, 28, 44
General Post Office (GPO) Tower, London, 34
Hall, Sir Benjamin, 27
Henry II, King, 19
Henry III, King, 40
Henry VIII, King, 40
Hugo, Victor, 20
Hunchback of Notre Dame, The, 20-22
Johnson Wax Research Tower, 30
Keep, 8
London, Tower of, 39-41
Marina Towers, 33
Mary, Queen, 40
Middle Ages, 14
Minaret, 16
Muezzin, 16
Nimrod, King, 13
Notre Dame Cathedral, 20
Old North Church Tower, 23
Oubliettes, 10
Peter II of Savoy, Duke, 43
Pisa, Leaning Tower of, 24
"Prisoner of Chillon, The," 43
Quasimodo, 20-22
Qutub Minar, 16
Revere, Paul, 23
Sears Tower, 36
Siege Tower, 14
Torture, 6, 40, 43, 44
Ulm Cathedral, 17
William the Conqueror, 39
Wright, Frank Lloyd, 30
Ziggurats, 13

Photo on page 7 courtesy of the Chicago Convention and Tourism Bureau
Photos on pages 9, 18, 26, 35, 39 courtesy of the British Tourist Authority
Photo on page 20 courtesy of the French Government Tourist Office
Photo on page 25 courtesy of the Italian Government Travel Office
Photo on page 31 courtesy of Johnson Wax
Photo on page 36 courtesy of Sears, Roebuck and Co.
Photo on page 38 courtesy of the Embassy of the German Democratic Republic